# ALL *NEW* TRICKS FOR TRAINERS

*Dave Arch*

**Recommended Resources**
**Amherst, Massachusetts**

Published by:   Recommended Resources
22 Amherst Road
Amherst, MA 01002
(800) 822-2801 (U.S. and Canada)
(413) 253-3488
(413) 253-3490 (Fax)
http://www.hrdpress.com

First Edition, First Printing

ISBN 0-87425-448-5

*Typesetting by Michele Anctil*
*Cover art and design by Jim Gill and Barb Betz*
*Editorial work by Suzanne Bay*

# Dedication

A special thank-you to Randall Johnson and Linda Klemstein of Lakewood Publications:

To Randall for your exceptional skill in the editing of my Tricks For Trainers column every month.

To Linda for your personal encouragement and continual support of innovative training.

# Table of Contents

# Table of Contents *(continued)*

# Foreword

Several nights ago, Dave Arch and I attended a magic show. As the audience watched the performers, I was reminded of just how innately curious we all are. I watched young and old, male and female—people from all walks of life—lean forward in their chairs, being pulled by such questions as "How does that work? What's going to happen next? What's the answer to that puzzle?" The mind's need for closure is so strong that once it's stirred by a paradox, it keeps working until it finds resolution.

Since Dave began as a Senior Training Consultant for Creative Training Techniques in 1994, I have watched him skillfully use the power of curiosity within simple magic tricks, easy-to-customize puzzles, and interactive games to draw participants deeper into his trainings. While he is a delightful presenter, he is also one of those individuals who can empower others towards greatness.

Whether your training position requires you to administer the same content over and over again, or train the same people session after session, you've already discovered the importance of finding a supply of quick and easy openers, closers, energizers, and review techniques to keep the presentations fresh for both you and your participants. Since I published Volume One of *Tricks for Trainers*, the collection has grown (with no duplication of material) to include Volume Two, three volumes of videos, and a monthly column in the *Creative Training Techniques Newsletter*. The training community's positive response over the years demonstrates the usefulness of Dave Arch's material. I am convinced that this book will prove to be no exception.

Whether you're looking for an opening to immediately grab the attention of your participants, a closing to memorably finish a session, or an intriguing review technique to help build higher content retention, you're sure to find many suitable activities within these covers. In the back of the book you'll also find a collection of some of the very best brain-teasing transparency masters from the Puzzlers for Presenters™ feature on the Creative Training Techniques web site (www.cttbobpike.com).

I would offer only two suggestions to effectively use these materials. You could easily find these activities so enjoyable that you succumb to the temptation to overuse them in your training. I would encourage you to consider these activities like salt in a well-seasoned food. A few sprinkled throughout your presentation will enhance the experience for your participants.

Be sure to apply each of your selected activities to your content. If you fail to do this, your participants will be preoccupied with such counter-productive questions as "Why did s/he do that? What was that all about?" or worse yet "That was a waste of time!" With the suggestions that Dave gives within each activity, finding content applications shouldn't be difficult at all.

My hope is that many of these activities find their way into your own training toolkit, as they have into mine.

Bob Pike
Editor, *The Creative Training Techniques Newsletter*
President, The Creative Training Techniques Companies

# Category Key

Use the key below to identify the icon that corresponds to a certain category.

 Opener

 Brain Game

 Perception Skills

 Listening Skills

 Involvement & Interaction

 Telepathic Trick

 Creative Tools

 Card Trick

 Competition

 Energizer

 Computer Skills

 Closing Technique

# Introduction

How do your participants expect you to open your training sessions? How do they expect you to close? How do they expect you to deliver your content in the body of the session? How do they expect you to review? These are important questions every trainer should ask . . . and answer.

Then . . . DON'T!

By that I mean, *don't* open the way they expect you to, *don't* close in the manner they've become accustomed to, *don't* play into their expectations if you desire to maximize their attention and retention! Have the courage to use the element of surprise and curiosity to keep positive energy flowing throughout the session.

Between the covers of this book you'll find 57 new ways to open, close, and energize training sessions, taken from my monthly "Tricks For Trainers" column in the *Creative Training Techniques Newsletter.*

My suggestions for using the book are quite simple. Rather than reading through the book from cover to cover, take just a moment to look at the Table of Contents and mark those chapter titles that pique your own interest.

As you go through the book and read the activities, take note of those that:

- *Sound like fun to you.* Only try those activities that you personally believe would be fun to facilitate. Your own enthusiasm for the activity will energize your participants, too!

- *Seem low risk for you.* Only try those activities that you can easily visualize using with your participants. You should have no trouble picturing them responding enthusiastically to the activity. Such positive visualization will greatly increase your confidence as you present the activity. Your confidence will then translate into greater buy-in on the part of your training group.

Then keep returning to the Table of Contents until you've found two or three activities that you'd like to try, based on the above criteria.

Finally, sprinkle one or two of the activities into your next training session. My belief is that once you see the positive response of your participants and sense your own revitalization because you have some new material to freshen your trainings, you'll come back for more.

And your participants will thank you, too!

Wishing you successful trainings,

Dave Arch
Senior Training Consultant
Creative Training Techniques International
darch@compuserve.com

P.S. Don't miss the final section of this book in which I share some of my Puzzlers for Presenters™ from our Creative Training Techniques web site (www.cttbobpike.com). If you make transparencies from these masters, you'll find yourself with some dynamic overheads for creating group discussion and energy at the beginning of a session or following a break!

# Openers & Energizers

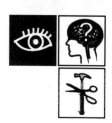

# 1

# Man Swims the Mississippi!

Collecting odd tabloid headlines is one of my more unusual hobbies. You know the kind I'm talking about—you see them in the supermarket all the time. I realize many of these are completely untrue; I collect the ones that only *sound* untrue. When you carefully read the story, you find out that the headline is accurate—just not in the same way that you first thought.

Here's an example of what I mean. Imagine seeing the headline: NEWSWEEK MAGAZINE FOLDS! Your first thought would probably be that the magazine had stopped publishing. You'd want to read the story to find out if that could possibly be true, and if so, why. However, when you get into the story itself, you would discover that the headline is referring to the publication physically folding in half! Your assumptions allowed you to be taken in by the sensational writing of the headline.

If you give your participants only a headline—from my collection or from your own—and then have them brainstorm the possible ways it could actually be true, you will have created a natural energizer. It's great for those "just back from lunch" moments when not quite everyone has returned and you want to get started, but you don't want to get into your main content because you'll just have to recap for late-comers.

You might try some of these:

**Man Falls off 120-Foot Ladder; Walks Away Unharmed!**

*Someone is sure to guess that he was only on the second rung of the ladder!*

**Woman Throws Herself through a 15th-Story Window and Lives!**

*Did you figure out that she was a window washer who actually threw herself into the window from the outside of the building? Someone else might suggest that it was even an inside window on the 15th floor (such as a window between offices).*

**Gioacchino Antonio Rossini Composed 50 Operas before his 11th Birthday!**

*This is actually true. However, what **isn't** in the headline is that the composer was born on February 29th of a leap year, and actually was 44 years old by the time he celebrated his 11th "birthday."*

Here's the most puzzling one I have in my collection:

**Man Becomes His Own Grandpa!**

*I was amazed. I had to read further. Here's the gist of what the story said: Tom married a widow who had a grown-up daughter. Tom's father married the widow's daughter. This made Tom's wife his own mother's (step-mother's) mother, which would make his wife his grandmother. If Tom is married to his own grandmother, then he must, indeed, be his own grandpa!*

I hope you have as much fun with these as I do. I know your participants will.

Incidentally, the headline on this item could be about a man who swims not the LENGTH of the Mississippi River, but its breadth.

# 2

# A Brain in Motion Stays in Motion

Are you familiar with what I affectionately call "group inertia"? It's that heaviness many groups experience as the instructor comes to the front of the room, ready to begin the training session. In many situations, group inertia will kill an otherwise successful opening. A wise trainer tries to head it off at the pass.

*Remember:* "inertia" applies not just to motion, but to lack of it. A moving object will continue to roll along until some force acts to stop it. A standing-still object—say, a roomful of parked brains—will stay put until something comes along to get things going.

My favorite inertia-breaking technique is to put a brain teaser on the overhead at least five minutes before the formal start of the session. I offer a prize to the first person or group who can solve it successfully.

That breaks up the inertia and gives me a running start. When the session formally begins, we aren't starting from a dead stop. Brain teasers that involve relationships are especially successful.

Try this one. Just show it on an overhead transparency (no interaction is necessary). Let students mull it over until you're ready to begin the session.

*A blind beggar had a brother who died, but the blind beggar was not the dead man's brother. How could this be? What relationship did the blind beggar have to the man who died?*

When your group figures out that the blind beggar was the dead man's sister, many applications present themselves, not the least of which is sexual stereotyping.

Here is another in the same genre:

*A man was overheard saying, "Brothers and sisters have I none, but that man's father is my father's son." What relationship did the man speaking have with the man he was referring to?*

The man speaking was actually the other man's father. Groups create a lot of energy trying to figure this one out. That energy translates into a stronger, more lively session start.

# 3

# Algebra in the A.M.

If you train highly technical people, you have probably noticed that your group finds these familiar "mind games" too simple to get excited about. They're an analytical group, and they really like mental challenges. Here's an "early-bird" activity that can be used before the session begins. It gets minds working, encourages interaction before the course is even under way, and sets the tone for what you promised from the outset would be a challenging and interesting program.

Copy the following onto a transparency and have students try to find the flaw in the equation. It is supposed to prove algebraically that we can all be any age we want to be:

YOU ARE THE AGE YOU WANT TO BE!

$a$ = future age you want to be
$n$ = the age you are now
$d$ = difference between the two ages

$a = n + d$
$a(a - n) = (n + d)(a - n)$
$a^2 - an = an + ad - n^2 - nd$
$a^2 - an - ad = an - n^2 - nd$
$a(a - n - d) = n(a - n - d)$
$a = n$

# 4

# Different Parts, Same Whole

Your students have more in common than they think. Emphasize the point at the start of any session with this number trick:

1.  Ask each member of your class to write down a three-digit number. The only rules are that the first and last numbers cannot be zero, and they cannot be the same.

2.  Ask participants to reverse the order of their numbers (792 becomes 297, for example) and then subtract the smaller number from the larger.

3.  If the result is 99 (as is the case when the original number is 819, for example), add a zero in the hundreds place (the new number in our example would be 099).

4.  Finally, ask students to add that number to the same number with its digits reversed.

Participants will be amazed to see they all have the same answer, regardless of the digits they chose: 1089.

<table>
<tr><td rowspan="5">Example</td><td>942</td></tr>
<tr><td>− 249</td></tr>
<tr><td>693</td></tr>
<tr><td>+ 396</td></tr>
<tr><td>1089</td></tr>
</table>

Use the exercise as a no-real-point attention-getter, or use it to focus the discussion on your message: No matter how different we are as individuals, everyone at the session has one thing in common. "We all have things to learn and things to teach one another—so let's get started!"

# 5

# The Customer Is Always (Drawn) First

When customer service is the *focus* of your training—and it's a focus in most sessions, if you think about it—here is a magical opener.

1.  Ask your participants, working in table teams, to list things that would prevent them from making and keeping customers the primary focus of their actions. They are to list as many hindrances as they can on index cards, one per card.

2.  The team then votes on the top five (or even three) hindrances, and shares those with the entire group. Those "best of" cards are collected by the trainer and dropped into a paper sack.

3.  A participant is then asked to draw a picture of a customer on another index card and drop it into the sack, as well. Another participant shakes the sack vigorously, mixing up the index cards.

4.  To illustrate the goal of the session, the trainer closes his or her eyes (or is even blindfolded for greater dramatic effect) and reaches into the sack. "This bag is full of difficulties, real problems, even a few excuses," he says, as he keeps his hand in the bag. But *this* must always come first!" With that, he withdraws the customer card, holding it high in the air.

*The secret:* When the trainer drops the cards in the sack, he bends the stack of cards strongly enough to put a crease in each card. (This severe crimp can either be width-wise or length-wise; since the participants never see these cards again, don't be afraid to REALLY BEND the cards.) All of this happens with one hand when that hand is out of sight and inside the sack with the cards. It only takes a second. The customer card is not bent; the trainer simply feels around inside the sack for the only unbent card. If this takes some time, it will only add to the suspense in the room.

This activity can be adapted to a wide range of topics where negatives or obstacles are involved. Ask students to list their own obstacles to better time management, cost control, and so on, and then create a card that represents the end goal that must be put ahead of all else.

*One note:* Make sure the stack of index cards is small enough so that you can bend it in half with one hand. A little experimentation should let you know how large the stack can be. If there are too many cards and you know it, be sure to put them into the sack in two or more groups so that they can all be bent.

# 6

# You've Got to Accentuate the Positive . . .

What training session wouldn't benefit from a clear comparison of positive versus negative behaviors, related to a course topic? The example below creates such a comparison. It comes from a train-the-trainer session, but the idea adapts easily with virtually any subject in which participants are able to identify positive and negative behaviors involving the topic.

The following is the narrative the trainer uses to deliver the "Three Traits" message:

"Before we begin, I need you to place on a table in front of you three small pieces of paper. Please print a number "1" on one piece of paper, a number "2" on another, and a number "3" on the third.

"On sheet number one, please write one characteristic of an *ineffective* training presentation. (Substitute "an ineffective sales presentation," "an unsuccessful speech," etc., according to your course topic.) On the second sheet, write a characteristic of an *effective* training presentation. On the sheet numbered three, write another characteristic of an ineffective training presentation.

"After you've finished, you can place them in any order. However, the three pieces of paper do need to be in a row. The order is completely up to you. You'll have to agree that there's no way I could possibly know which paper is in which position. Now, we're going to mix them up as I give you some brief instructions. All I ask is that you follow my instructions carefully, one step at a time:

1. Exchange the piece of paper on which you wrote a number "1" with the paper on its immediate right. If there is no paper on its immediate right, just leave the paper with number 1 on it alone.

2. Exchange the paper on which you wrote a number 2 with the paper on its immediate left. If there is no paper on its immediate left, just leave the paper with the number 2 on it alone.

3.  Exchange the paper on which you wrote a number 3 with the paper on its immediate right. If there is no paper on its right, just leave the paper with the number 3 on it alone. You have now mixed up the papers.

4.  Slowly let your hand pass over the row of papers from one end to the other and back again, not touching the papers but casting a shadow over all three. Let your hand come down slowly on the paper in the middle of the row. Grab it, wad it up, and throw it away. This represents a quality we're trying to eliminate.

5.  Only two remain. Again, let your hand slowly move over the remaining papers and let it come down on top of the paper on the right. Grab it, wad it up, and throw it away. We're working to eliminate this, too.

Congratulations! You have successfully retained an important quality for an effective presentation, while eliminating those qualities that hinder effectiveness."

# Learner Motivation

# 7

# You Don't Know "Jacks"

If your company does not allow participants to "test" out of your courses or if you're called upon to teach mandatory sessions, you have undoubtedly crossed paths with that problematic participant I refer to as the "Know-It-All."

Whether the participant actually does know it all or doesn't know it all is not the issue. The fact that this person *believes* that he or she knows it all creates a participant with an attitude.

I want to share with you an exercise that helps neutralize the effect such a participant can have on a class. In preparation for the activity, you'll need to have the face cards from a deck of playing cards at each training table.

Humorously tell your participants that they have exactly four minutes to carefully examine the faces of each of the cards before a "test" is administered.

When the time limit expires, pose the following questions:

1. How many kings wear mustaches?

2. How many kings face left?

3. How many kings carry battle-axes?

4. How many kings hold their swords upright?

5. How many kings have both hands showing?

6. How many kings wear beards?

7. What do the queens hold in their hands?

8. How many queens face to the right?

9. How many queens have dimples in their cheeks?

10. How many jacks wear mustaches?

11. How many jacks face to the left?

12. How many one-eyed jacks are there?

13. Do all the jacks have curly hair?

14. Each jack wears a hat. What color are the hats?

The exercise can be made simpler by using fewer face cards or simply by asking fewer questions. The follow-up discussion is the same, regardless: How many times do you believe you have seen a face card in your lifetime? How would you define the difference between seeing and really observing? What components made this activity so difficult? What could have been done to make each person more successful on the test? How do you believe the results might change if we did the activity again? Why?

As you can see, this activity can be spun in a number of different directions. There are lessons for everyone in the room. For the sake of our know-it-alls, though, point out this lesson:

> *We can see something many times—to the point of total familiarity, perhaps—and still not learn some fairly basic things about the subject. It is truly amazing how we can LOOK AT something and still not really SEE it.*

In a fun and interactive manner, you've helped make that point to those who are familiar with your content. These participants will be challenged to look at that content from a completely new perspective, and will be amazed at what they discover!

# 8

# Stump the Trunk

I like to play a game I call "stump the trunk." It's easy: All you have to do is develop or learn a handful of prop-based learning demonstrations, and then carry those props to your training sessions in a small box or "trunk."

The rules are simple: Someone from the audience suggests a content area that they find difficult to make interactive and lively for their participants. I then look through my trunk of training props, attempting to find an activity that might help them energize their content.

A gentleman in one of my sessions wondered if I had anything that might serve as a fun closing for a training session on ISO 14000. That was a new one for me. Staring down into my prop trunk for a minute or so, I finally grabbed a deck of playing cards and made a suggestion. I think you'll see why this closing can be easily customized to just about any topic:

*The man came to the front of the room and shuffled the deck of playing cards. Then, while my back was turned, he did two things. He looked at and remembered a card in the deck and noted how many cards down it was from the top of the face-down deck. Then he showed the card to the audience.*

*I turned back around and took the deck from him, placing the deck behind my back. I told him I was attempting to find his card, and move it to a new location in the deck. I brought the face-down deck out from behind my back and asked him how many cards down in the deck his card was originally. He told me that it was 14 cards down.*

*We counted 14 cards down and put those cards aside. His card was no longer in that position. I told him that it was no longer there because I had successfully found it and moved it. The entire audience then spelled aloud the phrase "ISO 14000" as I removed one card from the face-down deck for each letter or digit. His card turned up on the final 0 of the 14000!*

This trick will work with any word or phrase! Here's how: Follow the scenario above, and when you put the deck behind your back, transfer from the bottom of the face-down deck to the top the same number of cards as there are letters in your summarizing word or phrase. (I transferred eight cards for the phrase "ISO 14000.")

Then continue to the conclusion of the presentation as described above, and you will find (possibly to your own amazement) that it works every time! In all probability, some of your participants will beg you to show them how it's done. However, I'd encourage you not to buckle under this pressure. Don't be afraid to tap into that most powerful training energy—participant curiosity. Wouldn't it be great to have participants start to say great things about you, such as, "When you take that course, be sure and ask to see that unbelievable card trick!"? That's great pre-session publicity. You could become a legend within your own training department.

# 9

# Magicians Among Us

A deck of cards for each table of participants and the following instructions are all you need for "Under the Spell," a card-trick that ends your session with a magical sense of energy.

Ten minutes before the close of your session, tell participants that you have a new card trick you'd like to try. Ask them to open the decks of cards at their tables, and divide the cards among group members.

Instruct participants to shuffle their cards. One person at each table then collects the stacks, shuffles the entire deck, and passes the deck to the person at their immediate left. (The person with the cards at this point becomes the first "volunteer" and continues with the steps that follow, until instructed to let another group member take charge.) No need for lots of memorization on your part—simply read the following instructions to the class, giving them time to perform each step:

1. Deal one card face-down onto the table for each letter of the phrase "pick me."

2. Look at the last card you deal, and show it to the others. Remember that card.

3. Put the card back down on the table pile, and drop the rest of the deck face-down on top of that pile. The person to the left now takes over.

4. Pick up the deck from the table, holding it face-down in your hand. Spell your full name onto the table, dealing one card with each letter.

5. Turn the portion of the deck still in your hand face-up and drop it on the pile of cards that now lie on the table. The person to the left takes over.

6. Without turning it over, pick up the deck from the table and spell your mother's full maiden name, dealing one card onto a table pile for each letter.

7.  Without turning it over, drop the deck from your hand onto the pile on the table. The person to the left takes over.

8.  Without turning it over, pick up the deck from the table and spell the name of the street on which you live.

9.  Turn the deck in your hand face-down and drop it on the table pile. The person to the left now takes over.

10. Volunteer number one: Identifies the card that was selected at the beginning of the trick. It's the job of the most recent volunteer to find that card. (Pause momentarily to create a sense of drama.)

11. Without turning it over, pick up the deck from the table and spell the word "magic," placing one card on the table for each letter.

12. The card that is now on top of the deck in the spectator's hand is the selected card. The volunteer holds it up for confirmation.

13. The participants—now members of an accomplished magic troupe—each take a bow.

# 10

# They'll Return on Time Like Magic!

Put simply, there's nothing like a gimmick to encourage participants to return from breaks on time. Here's one that's sure to bring them back.

Issue the following challenge to your participants: "Immediately following break, I will attempt a most unbelievable card trick. After a deck of cards is thoroughly shuffled, I will place it in my pocket. The group can then choose any card in the deck, and I will reach into my pocket and attempt to find—by touch alone—a card or cards that add up to the number on the group's selected card. The last card I pull from my pocket will match your chosen card's suit."

Trust me. They will be back from break on time.

Before you attempt this trick, however, secretly place in your pocket the following cards: Ace of clubs, two of hearts, four of spades, eight of diamonds—in that order. Use the word CHaSeD to remember the order of the suits (clubs, hearts, spades, diamonds). The numbers of the cards are merely double with each card.

Those four cards should remain hidden in your pocket. When your participants return from break, divide up the remainder of the deck among the participants. Ask them to shuffle their cards. Reassemble the deck and remind students of your challenge.

Put the deck in your pocket. Ask the group to select any card in the deck (except the joker) and then call out their decision. Repeat your declaration that you will attempt to pull cards from your pocket whose values equal that of the card they named—11 for the Jack, 12 for the Queen, 13 for the King— and that you hope the last card you pull will match the suit they have chosen.

By using the words "attempt" and "hope" in your description, you will suggest a certain potential for failure that will only add to the impact on your participants when you ultimately succeed.

Put the shuffled deck in your pocket next to the four cards already there. In other words, the four previously-arranged cards will now either be on the top or the bottom of the shuffled deck.

Now let's imagine the group deciding to challenge you with the five of diamonds.

After suitable concentration and some silent mental figuring (take all the time you need to think—remember, you're supposed to make this look difficult), you reach into your pocket and remove the Ace of clubs. That counts as "one." Then dip into the pocket again and come out with the four of spades. That counts for "four," bringing your total now up to the "five."

However, you still don't have the suit. So, as promised, reach into the pocket and bring out the eight of diamonds; that should satisfy the crowd that you have now matched the suit. (If the class had named the five of clubs, you could have first drawn the four of spades from your pocket, followed by the Ace of clubs.)

Unlike most magic tricks, this one seems to grow in popularity with repetition. Although I would never do this trick more than twice for the same group (people might start realizing you draw from a bank of four cards after a few repetitions), don't be afraid to do it two times. You can get people back on time for three breaks: the first, when you perform the trick; the second, when you repeat it; and the third, when you promise to reveal the secret.

After explaining how the trick works, you may be able to apply it to the course topic. Ask questions like:

*What process do you suppose the inventor of this trick had to go through to determine the minimum number of cards needed to accomplish the challenge?*

*How is the inventor's process similar to what any organization must go through to get the most results from limited resources (i.e., budget, personnel, time, etc.)?*

*Are there tasks you can accomplish more efficiently by applying old tools in new and creative ways?*

This activity will underscore the importance of creativity in achieving results with limited resources. If you use it, you will demonstrate the possibility of such an achievement, and you will keep a session running on schedule for one full day with the help of a single card trick!

# 11

# Three Possible Impossibilities

Participants about to undergo training often worry about their ability to master the content. Here is a collection of three "impossible" assignments you can use to teach students that a task is much easier to accomplish IF YOU KNOW HOW.

A.  Did you know that you can break unbreakable fishing line (or thread) with the right training? Distribute several 12-inch pieces of nylon fishing line. Purchase heavy-enough line so that no one in your group will be able to break it with their bare hands. Eight-pound fishing line should be acceptable for the exercise.

Give participants a chance to try and break the line. They won't be able to do so. Then have them follow directions as you model this process for breaking that fishing line easily:

1.  Wrap the line several times around the index finger of your left hand.

2.  From the index finger, bring the strand down into the palm of your left hand. Leave slack there, creating a sort of loop on your palm.

3.  Bring the remainder of the line up through the space between your thumb and index finger, taking care to leave the "loop" in your palm.

4.  Pass the strand down the back of your hand and back to the front of your hand. Thread it through the "loop" in your palm.

5.  Wrap your right hand around the fishing line hanging below your left hand and close both hands. Put your hands close together and pull. You will be amazed to see how easily the fishing line breaks. It actually cuts itself!

**B.** Challenge participants to drink out of a glass without using a straw or their hands, and without putting their noses into the glass.

Pass out clear plastic cups, fill each with a little water, and give students some time to struggle with the exercise. It's not likely they'll come up with your solution, so after a while, show them how it's done:

Put your lips over the far rim of the cup so that your nose is to the outside of the glass. Tip the liquid forward into your mouth as you lean forward (almost standing on your head, really). It's a riot to watch, and great fun for students to try.

**C.** Challenge a class volunteer to a drinking race. On the table in front of the room, set up three full-size glasses and three shot glasses, and fill each with soda. The challenge is this: The three full-size glasses are yours and the three shot glasses belong to the participant. You will challenge the participant to drink the beverages faster than you.

As impossible as it seems, you tell the group that you will finish drinking the three large glasses of soda before the challenger finishes drinking the soda in the three shot glasses. The only rule is that you can't touch the challenger's glasses and he or she can't touch yours. Seems fair? Seems impossible!

After starting the race on the count of three, drink your first soda and (with your now-empty glass) calmly cover his last full shot glass. You'll win. Remember: your opponent can't touch any of your glasses! Calmly finish off the remaining glasses at your leisure throughout the rest of your training.

The impossible will again have been made possible with a little creativity and a little training. And the *best* part is that your participants will take these tricks outside the classroom and try them on friends and colleagues, remembering and sharing with others the enjoyable time they had in your training session. Learner motivation and great advertising for your future sessions!

# 12

# The Magic Flame and the Hankie

When participants have completed the course and you're ready to send them back to the job, they always harbor a little spark of apprehension about whether or not they will be able to successfully implement what they've learned.

Sometimes we trainers overlook, in our content planning, the fact that it takes courage on the part of participants to take what we offer them and actually use it to effect CHANGE in their comfortable, established working environments.

Consequently, the last moments of a session are a great time for a little motivational input, in the form of a closing ceremony.

Make sure that you've already collected course evaluations, cleaned up the room, and handled any other housekeeping chores you might have before going into the presentation. (If you don't take care of these things ahead of time, you will just kill this closing.) When you're done with this little object lesson, the only thing left for the participants to do is leave the room.

You'll need a cigarette lighter and a fairly large men's handkerchief. Have two participants come to the front of the room and have each one hold the handkerchief by two corners so that it is held out flat in front of you. Stand between the two participants, holding the lighter as you speak:

"Anytime we go back to the job with the anticipation of trying something new, there is a little apprehension. 'Will I succeed? Will I fail?' are always questions on our minds. I would only remind you that, as we look back over our lives, most of the things we've worried about never happened. Most of the times that we thought something terrible was going to take place, it turned out to not be nearly as bad as we feared."

At this point, ignite the lighter so that the flame burns for the remainder of your presentation. Slowly move the lighter toward the back of the handkerchief.

Of course, your participants are expecting to see the handkerchief burst into flames. Instead, you bring the flame right up to the rear edge of the handkerchief so that the blue part of the flame meets the edge, and the colored part of the flame extends above the handkerchief.

Keep moving the lighter so that it's underneath the handkerchief, close to the fabric. Here's the secret of the phenomenon: The blue part of the flame is cooler than the rest and it's the only part that is in contact with the fabric, so the handkerchief *will not burn*!

Instead, the flame will extend above the handkerchief (through the cloth) and will move in response to the movement of the lighter underneath. Keep the lighter moving: Don't hold it in one place! Keep the lighter tightly against the fabric underneath the handkerchief, and you (and your assistants) will be amazed to see that the cloth is not burning at all.

When you're done moving the flame around the material, slide the lighter out from underneath the handkerchief and keep the flame burning while you say something like this:

> *"With a little courage and the skills you've acquired during this course, you will find success back on the job. (Look at the still-burning flame as you say this last line.) You'll find that your courage will reap many rewards and that all will work out better than you can even anticipate sitting here in this classroom."* (Look at the lighter and extinguish the flame.)

Thank your two assistants for holding the handkerchief, retrieve it from them, and thank all your participants for taking the class.

# 13

# Calculator "Connivery"

During computer training sessions—especially those designed for computer beginners—a trainer is sometimes needed just to lower anxiety levels. Here is a fun computer trick to teach your students. It will help familiarize them with the calculator function of their computer, and they will enjoy showing the trick to their friends and co-workers. (This can be demonstrated with hand-held calculators, as well.)

If you'd like it to serve as a problem-solving exercise, demonstrate the trick for course participants (without telling them how to do it) and have the class brainstorm how you pulled it off. Give a prize to the first person who comes up with the solution. You can demonstrate the trick several times throughout the day while class members look for clues that will tell them how it's done.

Here's how to do the trick:

1. Secretly enter the calculator mode of your computer and type in the equation 68888889 + 1. Do NOT hit the equals button at this point. You will find that now your screen only shows the number "1." The class should be unaware of the previous number you entered into the computer.

2. Here's where the trick begins, as far as attendees are concerned. Show the class the number "1" on your computer screen. Leave the "1" showing, and continue by entering the number 2345678. Now your calculator will show the number 12345678.

3. Mention to your participants that you are about to show them a little known quirk about the calculator function on a computer. Remind them, with a smirk, that you are a trained professional, and that they probably shouldn't try this at home.

   Gently reach up with whichever hand is least conspicuous and tap your monitor on the right side. What students don't realize is that at the same time you tap on the side of your monitor, you are also pushing on the "=" button on your keyboard. They will be amazed to see on the display that your tap has apparently knocked the eight from the right end of the row to the far left end of the row. The number on your display will read 81234567.

The trick can serve as a nice break from more serious training throughout the day. Make sure you laugh while you're doing it, and explain as you go along that computers can be a lot of fun, if you let them.

If no one catches on to you, show them how the trick is done at the end of the day. Beginning computer users will be excited to know a bit of computer "magic" they can use to impress their more computer-savvy friends.

# Communications

# 14

# Same Words, Different Message

Precision in written communication is becoming increasingly important. With e-mail substituting for telephone conversations or face-to-face meetings, this is a great time to make that point again. Here's an activity that does so in a humorous, memorable manner.

Take the following unpunctuated e-mail and transfer it onto an overhead transparency. (Make two transparencies with the same text on each.) Give two copies of the paragraph to each participant.

> Dear Tom I want a man who knows what love is all about you are generous kind thoughtful people who are not like you admit to being useless and inferior you have ruined me for other men I yearn for you I have no feelings whatsoever when we're apart I can be forever happy will you let me be yours Sheila

Tell participants that Sheila is madly in love with Tom and wants to communicate her love through e-mail. However, the group will need to punctuate the letter, so Tom can really feel Sheila's emotions.

Give them a few moments to do that. Then have someone read the results aloud to the rest of the group.

It will probably sound something like this:

*Dear Tom,*
*I want a man who knows what love is all about. You are generous, kind,*
*thoughtful. People who are not like you admit to being useless and inferior.*
*You have ruined me for other men. I yearn for you. I have no feelings whatsoever*
*when we're apart. I can be forever happy. Will you let me be yours?*
*Sheila*

As the person reads it aloud, you can punctuate it on the overhead.

Tell the class that shortly thereafter, Tom offended Sheila in a major way (no need to go into the sordid details) and she wanted to dump him big-time. Amazingly enough, she found she could use the same letter to get rid of Tom. She just needed to punctuate it a little differently.

Give them time to work on their second copy of the letter to try and communicate Sheila's hostility towards Tom.

This second exercise may be a little harder to do, but the end result is truly hilarious. The finished version will read something like this:

*Dear Tom,*
*I want a man who knows what love is. All about you are generous, kind,*
*thoughtful people who are not like you. Admit to being useless and inferior.*
*You have ruined me. For other men I yearn. For you I have no feelings*
*whatsoever. When we're apart I can be forever happy. Will you let me be?*
*Yours,*
*Sheila*

Even the most punctuation-indifferent participants will be forced to acknowledge that a comma has the power to change lives. With that point made, your audience should be ready for messages about grammar and usage, careful composition, use of e-mail systems, or just about any lesson in written communication you'd like to deliver.

# 15

# Emphasize That That, Not This That

Since participants never bring an unlimited supply of energy into our training sessions, the wise trainer always keeps a few energizers on hand. The best examples actually boost the energy level of participants. Here's one I'd like to share that has been consistently successful every time I've used it in a training session. It's a wonderful lesson in clear communication, too!

This series of sentences can be transferred to a transparency. Show the sentences one at a time and offer a prize to the first person who can read each sentence aloud with pauses and inflections that make the sentence understandable to the group.

You'll find, at first, that everyone will be mumbling to themselves, trying to make sense out of the sentences. Someone will eventually hazard a guess. As the exercise catches on, the room will fill with energy and, in just a few minutes, groggy students will awaken and be ready to re-focus on your content.

Here's the first series:

1. **"He said that that that that that woman said should have been which."**

   After struggling for a while, someone is sure to deduce that the sentence is really:

   *"He said that that 'that' that that woman said should have been 'which.'"*

   After discovering the pattern, the second one becomes easier.

2. **"It was and I said not but."**

   The punctuation that helps this reading is: *"It was 'and' I said, not 'but.'"*

As a conclusion to this energizer, have your entire training group read the following in unison. It brings humorous closure to this activity.

> "Esau Wood saw a saw saw wood as no other wood saw Wood saw would saw wood. Of all the wood saws Wood ever saw saw wood Wood never saw a wood saw that would saw wood as the wood saw Wood saw saw wood would saw wood and I never saw a wood saw that would saw wood as the wood saw Wood saw would saw until I saw Wood saw wood with the wood saw Esau Wood saw saw wood."

Your participants will laugh out loud throughout the exercise and then breathe a sigh of relief when they successfully complete the reading. And that's good energy for a training session!

# 16

# Father's Cousin's Sister's Son

"Relational" riddles are versatile tools. They teach about communication clarity and the importance of detail. They grab a group's full attention—always useful, especially if you're working up to a particularly vital training moment. *And* they're entertaining.

Here's an example:

A woman was overheard saying,

"That person's mother was my mother's mother-in-law."

What relation is the lady who is speaking to the person she's talking about?

The lady speaking is the daughter of the person about whom she is speaking. It sure is a complicated way to say it, but it provides us with a good, if exaggerated, illustration of how we can complicate our communications through clumsy or confusing language.

"I'm My Own Grandpa" has to be one of the greatest relational songs of all time. The song tells the story of a man who wakes up to discover that through his marriage and his wife's relations, he has actually become his own grandpa. If you can find a recording, you might have some fun with it in a future session.

Here's a challenging brain teaser along the same lines that makes an entertaining course opener. Put it on a transparency and give your group five minutes to discuss and solve it before you begin your presentation. You'll be amazed at the energy it generates and the head start it gives you when you actually begin your training session.

> The first speaker says, "I am the same relation to Bobby as Bobby is to you."
>
> The second speaker replies, "I am the same relationship to you as Bobby is to your father."

What relationship do the two speakers have to one another?

They'll have to work on this one. Don't be afraid to hold out for a while with the answer. Think about saving the answer for closing comments before the first break, or for the first remarks when the group returns from that break. By maintaining the tension, you'll find the exercise heightens the group's energy even more.

*The solution:* The first speaker is the second speaker's grandfather. Bobby is the second speaker's father and the first speaker's son.

# 17

# Detail Counts—Period

When I'm working with a group to improve written communication skills, I'll often put the following on an overhead transparency for participants to work on immediately after returning from a break:

"A mother elephant had two babies named Samson and Delilah. What is the name of the mother."

There is enough information in the above statement to give you the name of the mother. Can you figure it out?

This activity really underscores the importance of attention to detail in our own written communication, as well as that of others. If you look back at the statement on the transparency, you will notice that there is no question mark at the end of the second sentence. The second sentence is actually a statement: "What" is the name of the mother.

Here is a similar exercise:

A fifth grade student, when asked to write a true story, wrote the following:

> ### A WALK IN THE PARK
>
> Last Sunday, when Sally went for a walk
> she saw a policeman skipping rope
> she saw a fire engine eating an ice-cream cone
> she saw a squirrel humming a tune
> she saw a puppy climbing a tree
> she saw two robins playing hopscotch
> she saw the sun shining brightly in the sky.

After reading the story, the teacher reprimanded the student for not writing a true story. "It isn't even partly believable," the teacher said. "Yes, it is," the student replied, and went on to prove that it was all completely believable. The teacher was forced to agree.

What did the student do to convince the teacher?

All the student did was punctuate the story as follows:

---

**A WALK IN THE PARK**

Last Sunday, when Sally went for a walk,
she saw a policeman; skipping rope,
she saw a fire engine; eating an ice-cream cone,
she saw a squirrel; humming a tune,
she saw a puppy; climbing a tree,
she saw two robins; playing hopscotch,
she saw the sun shining brightly in the sky.

---

When using this exercise, I display the unpunctuated version on the overhead as participants enter the training room. I might have it typed in a font that makes it look like a child's handwriting in order to give it personality.

I start the session by telling the story about the student and the teacher, and spend a few minutes letting students brainstorm about how the girl changed her teacher's mind.

Adding the punctuation usually makes quite an impact; students can see how important it is to pay attention to written details. I hope you have as much fun with it as I have.

# 18

# Laughable Ads, Laudable Learning

Written correspondence, the only means of long-distance communication for centuries, declined sharply after the invention of the telephone. E-mail has brought even more changes and, in many cases, has made employers increasingly aware that the writing skills of their employees are a little rusty. Quick and immediate communication made possible by computers only exacerbates the problem.

I use classified ads—some real, some created with a bit of license on my part—to illustrate in a humorous way what happens when words are put together quickly and carelessly. Here are a few examples:

- Now is your chance to get your ears pierced and get an extra pair to take home too!

- Tired of cleaning yourself? Let me do it!

- Dog For Sale. Eats anything and especially fond of children.

- New Restaurant Prices! Turkey $4.75 Chicken $4.50 Children $2.00

- Vacation Paradise. View Mt. Kilimanjaro from the Serena Lodge. Swim in the lovely pool while you drink it all in.

- For Rent! Six room hated apartment.

- Used Cars! Why go elsewhere to be cheated? Come here first!

- Three-year-old teacher needed for preschool. Experience preferred.

- Auto Repair Service. Free pick-up and delivery. Try us once, and you'll never go anywhere again.

- Visit the Superstore! Unequaled in size, unmatched in variety, unrivaled inconvenience.

By analyzing each example, you can identify some of the most common mistakes made in written communication. Let your participants identify what those mistakes are as they attempt to re-write each ad so that it makes sense.

(Or you might just want to put the collection on a transparency and use it as a great come-back-from-break/lunch activity before you dive back into your content.)

# 19

# Eliminate Jargon ASAP

Jargon. Every industry uses it. Sometimes I stand in the front of the training room and let participants pepper me with the jargon of their particular industry. I'm always amazed at how glibly they can call out numerous terms and acronyms that obviously have a lot of meaning to them but mean absolutely nothing to me.

Although jargon makes communicating more efficient within a particular corporate culture, it certainly does not make it easy for new employees. Consequently, within the training room, jargon must be used only after carefully defining the terms for participants new to the system.

Here's a fun way to make that point: Take the paragraph that follows and place it on a transparency, so that you can show it to the entire room.

> "When promulgating your esoteric cogitations or articulating your superficial sentimentalities and amicable philosophical and psychological observations, beware of platitudinous ponderosity. Let your verbal evaporations have lucidity, intelligibility and veracious vivacity without rodomontade or thespian bombast. Sedulously avoid all polysyllabic profundity, pompous propensity and sophomoric vacuity."

Let students try to tell you what the paragraph means; offer a prize to anyone who successfully translates it.

Actually, the entire paragraph means: "Don't use big words." Your participants will laugh when they learn how simply the message could have been delivered—and your point will be immediately understood.

I used another method to make the same point at a recent session on interactive distance learning (which has its own unique set of technical jargon). I had three decks of word cards on the front table. These were made from index cards, with the following words on each set, one per card:

| Deck 1 Words | Deck 2 Words | Deck 3 Words |
|---|---|---|
| Sequential | Creative | Resources |
| Homogeneous | Effectiveness | Concept |
| Social | Involvement | Objectives |
| Environmental | Culture | Adjustment |
| Interdependent | Maturation | Evaluation |
| Perceptual | Motivation | Activity |
| Incremental | Relationship | Capacity |
| Exceptional | Integration | Processes |
| Developmental | Accelerated | Curriculum |
| Instructional | Orientation | Utilization |
| Professional | Cognitive | |

*Here's how to use the cards:* Each of three volunteers draws a random card from the first deck, one from the second deck, and one from the third deck. Their task is to incorporate the resulting phrase into a highly intelligent-sounding statement about distance learning.

For instance, one of my students drew the words "homogenous" (deck 1) "effectiveness" (deck 2) and "objectives" (deck 3). Her intelligent-sounding statement: "Before designing curriculum for distance learning, the instructional designer must establish very specific homogenous effectiveness objectives."

You get the idea. After your three volunteers have completed their sentences, give them small prizes. Ceremoniously put away all the cards, making a statement (now that we've gotten THAT out of our systems) that you are banning technical jargon for the rest of the session.

In spite of that admonition, I have used the game in groups where participants would beg me to bring out the cards for another round. If you find jargon slipping into the conversation, you might try squelching it by making violators perform the task again, as an ongoing reminder that there is a time and a place for jargon, but this isn't it.

# Delivery

# 20

# "Step" Carefully

The prospect of creatively teaching a step-by-step process strikes terror in most trainers' hearts. It's so difficult to make process training interactive, to step away from the lecture-based format. Teaching the steps isn't the hard part, actually: Teaching the POINT of the steps is. That's doubly true if you're teaching a new process for an old job and your main competition is "the way it's always been done."

I like to make a case for "process" in a situation like this using the opener that follows. The method dramatically underscores what can be accomplished by thoroughly understanding a process and then adhering to that process, and highlights the potential for a new process to out-perform the tried-and-true older way of getting things done.

I don't explain the process the first time around, but assure the group that I will before the end of the session. I generally use it once or twice during the day as an energizer and when I want to heighten anticipation for the moment when THE SECRET is uncovered at day's end.

Begin by preparing four strips of card stock large enough to be seen by everyone in your room (suggested size 4 inches wide by 12 inches long). Each strip contains a column of evenly spaced numbers printed vertically on the front, and then on the back.

|          | Front | Back |
|----------|-------|------|
| Card #1  | 9     | 3    |
|          | 1     | 8    |
|          | 5     | 6    |
|          | 4     | 4    |
|          | 2     | 7    |
| Card #2  | 5     | 1    |
|          | 0     | 5    |
|          | 2     | 4    |
|          | 6     | 7    |
|          | 7     | 8    |

*(continued)*

| Card #3 | 4 | 6 |
|---|---|---|
| | 3 | 4 |
| | 8 | 2 |
| | 6 | 7 |
| | 2 | 5 |
| Card #4 | 2 | 8 |
| | 2 | 7 |
| | 3 | 1 |
| | 9 | 7 |
| | 6 | 4 |

If you wish to teach your participants this trick, you can prepare a set for them using 8½" × 11" sheets of card stock. The strips can be cut by participants and used with friends and co-workers after the class. If preparation time is at a premium, distribute sheets of card stock and have students make their own cards from your patterns.

Introduce this training trick with talk of a challenge. You are going to pit your mind against all the calculators and computers in the room. Here are the steps:

1.  Invite a participant to the front of the room and show him or her the four strips of numbers, both front and back. The volunteer is invited to arrange the strips side-by-side on the tray of the flipchart easel, in any order with any side facing out.

    If these cards were arranged in a row, you would have essentially created a random addition problem of five four-digit numbers.

    For example:

    9 1 4 8
    1 5 3 7
    5 4 8 1
    4 7 6 7
    2 8 2 4

    By allowing the participant to arrange the strips with any side facing out, it is apparent that there are literally hundreds of different combinations possible.

2.  After the volunteer places the strips, you will attempt to add the five four-digit numbers faster than anyone in the room. Appoint a time-keeper and begin.

3.  While the other participants feverishly type the numbers into their computers or calculators, you calmly pick up a piece of paper and a pen. Holding the paper so that only you can see what you're writing, you print the digits 22220. Underneath that, print the second row of numbers in the arrangement on the flip chart easel's tray. For the example above, the second row of numbers would be 1537.

Consequently, your paper now looks like this:    22220
                                                  1537

Add those two numbers together, arriving at a total of 23757.

You've just found the same answer you would have if you had laboriously added all those five-digit numbers in the traditional manner. (Don't make it appear too easy. Struggle a little to add drama to the competition.)

5.  Each time you perform this demonstration, you will merely add the second row of numbers to the number 22220. You will arrive at the answer before others have even entered the numbers in their calculators and computers, and there's virtually no chance they'll stumble upon your "process."

6.  Each time you apply the demonstration, weave the importance of process into the discussion. Explain how the common process works well enough, but clearly not as well as your new process. Explain that yours is as meticulous as theirs and that every step is essential, but that there is simply a better process than the ones they are using.

Ask students to discuss and agree upon the importance of process when tackling a problem. Ask them to consider if a new process might possibly be an improvement over the time-tested methods they know and practice. Have them discuss the benefits of learning a new way of doing something, rather than merely remaining with the familiar.

When you see your participants eagerly cutting out their own strips of numbers and practicing the trick with a co-worker in the training room, bask in the assurance that you have made your point about process. As they take this simple trick outside the walls of the training room to show others, the transfer of learning will be enhanced.

# 21

## Memo Magic

A good closing will leave people talking about your course for a long time to come. Here's one I use that puts students in awe and gets them excited about sharing their training experiences with people who were not there.

Unlike most Tricks for Trainers, this technique requires an additional purchase, but I believe you'll find the impact worth the small investment. The device is useful not just for this exercise, but for daily use, when you wish to make verbal notes to yourself. If you don't already own a memo recorder, you can get one relatively inexpensively at office stores, discount stores, and perhaps even in a toy department. Any model will do, with one important caveat: It *must* have a fast-forward button. (Outside of class, you can actually use the recording device to help remember important information.) The button will skip from one recorded message to the next, instantly. (I use the brand name "Voice It." Mine holds up to nine messages, but the more expensive ones will hold even more.)

*Prior to the presentation,* make a series of recordings, one for each major content point, using a small memo recorder. Record them in the order of your presentation so that you will know how many times you'll need to press the fast-forward button to get to the correct prediction.

*At the beginning of the presentation,* the presenter hands a sealed envelope to someone sitting in the front row for safekeeping. "We'll get to that later," is all the presenter says, loud enough for everyone to hear.

*After finishing the presentation,* you (the presenter) remind the audience of the envelope. Ask any participant to stand and freely call out any of the major points emphasized during the presentation.

*After the participant announces their selection,* go to the person in the front row and take the envelope. Open it and show the device. Ask the person who made the selection to come forward (select someone sitting in the back of the room). While the volunteer is coming to the front, push the fast-forward button the correct number of times to get to the appropriate prediction. Have the person who made the selection push the play button. The recording will magically match up.

*After a volunteer identifies one of the main points,* the envelope is opened, revealing the memo devices. The presenter holds the device (to the microphone, if there is one), so everyone can hear the message, and presses the "play" button. It's the presenter's own voice, predicting the exact content emphasis just selected by the participant.

*The presenter takes a bow and the session ends* on an energized (and mysterious) note.

# 22

# "In Closing" Closes Brains

Closing a session involves a lot more than simply attaching the words "In summary" to your last paragraph. In fact, these and similar expressions are not particularly effective for wrap-ups. Here are two tips for making your closings interesting and informative without sending any signals that cut short your students' sensory intake:

- Do not use the words "In closing," "To summarize," or "One last time before we go." Your participants will surely shut their minds at the sound of those words. Instead of saying anything, just close.

- Take care of any housekeeping chores, collection of evaluations, and announcements beforehand. Then you won't be stepping on your own closing. When you are done with your closing, you'll simply say "good-bye" and that will be that.

If you follow these two suggestions, your closing will be much more effective.

# 23

# The Mysterious Main Messages

The trainer has an odd sheet of what looks like hieroglyphics hanging in the front of the room throughout the session. Several times during the day, participants have asked about it. But all the trainer will tell them is that it will be used later in the day.

At the conclusion of the day, the trainer does, indeed, take the weird sheet off the wall and (after making several quick folds) reveals that the puzzling words spell out a word summary for the course! Participants usually react in astonishment as the message comes into view.

1.  To prepare for this fun closing, take an 8½" × 11" sheet of paper and fold it vertically into four long columns. (The creases will be 11" long.) As you look down at the paper, we will call the first crease A, then crease B, and finally C.

2.  Fold the paper so that Crease C comes over and meets crease A. (This will happen thanks to crease B.)

3.  On the paper folded as above, use a felt marker to print a key content summary word (i.e. Safety, Quality, Customer, etc.). Position the word vertically, ***writing on the creases*** so that some of every letter is to the left of crease A and some of each letter is to the right of crease C.

4.  Now unfold the paper and use your marker to disguise what you've just done by filling the paper between what now looks like random marks with other truly random marks. Eventually, your unfolded paper will look like a sheet of indiscernible hieroglyphics.

5.  Hang this up in your room to draw curious inquiries from your participants. (To be even more deceptive, make a copy and hang that in the room. Then your creases won't even be present.)

6.  At the conclusion of the training session, take the sheet of hieroglyphics and fold it so that crease C again touches crease A, and it will reveal your summarizing word.

(Better yet, before closing, pass out copies of your unreadable hieroglyphics so that everyone in the class can do the folding and discover the message right along with you. Participants will take their copies home and show others—you will have built in an element for training transfer.)

# 24

# Carefully Calculated Words

All you need is a calculator (the older and cheaper the better) to impress your students with the following numbers game. It's perfect when you want to convey the importance of following directions to the letter, or when you want to make the point that things aren't always what they seem. But feel free to use it as a diversional energizer at any point in any session.

The basis of this activity is the fact that certain numbers on early calculators or on cheaper modern ones appear as letters when inverted. Below is a chart of numbers and their corresponding inverted letters.

| | | |
|---|---|---|
| 1 = I | 4 = H | 8 = B |
| 2 = Z | 5 = S | 9 = G |
| 3 = E | 7 = L | 0 = O |

On newer or more expensive calculators, the numbers aren't as blocky and thus don't resemble specific letters of the alphabet. This is one of those rare occasions when worse is actually better, but, that should not present a problem, since there are many cheaper, older calculators still in circulation.

You can ask people to take out their calculators and do a quick scan of the room to find a person whose calculator looks like it meets your low-tech needs, or you can simply supply one of your own and pass it to a volunteer at the start of the demonstration. Ideally, everyone will have a calculator and can do the exercises simultaneously, but if that's not possible, one or several students can do the exercises and share their results with the class.

To make your point (or to give your students a break from a long stretch of brainwork), use any of the following examples:

A.  "I'm thinking of a city in Idaho. It has a population of 30,000 (so ask the volunteer to enter that number in the calculator); the speed limit is 55 mph (the volunteer adds the number 55 to the previous entry), the highest mountain in the state is 5,000 feet (add 5,000), and the best steak dinner in this city costs $53.00 (add 53 to the total). Your inverted answer will tell you the city of which I'm thinking."

Here's another one:

B. "The company is using a new testing procedure to determine who's eligible for a position with the firm. Take a calculator and add together the numbers 37 + 81 + 91 + 73. Does your answer look the same even when it's inverted? It should! Good. That's the eye test.

"Now put the same numbers in the calculator without the plus (+) signs. You will have the numbers 37819173 on the screen. This is only to see if you can follow directions. Spin your calculator around to see if you're eligible for a position."

Try one more:

C. "Assume for a moment that you make $938 per year. Enter that figure into a calculator and turn it around to see what you'd need to do in order to make ends meet. Let's assume you received a raise of $5055 for the year. Add that to your first figure to see what you could now afford to buy. Finally, add $26,015 to reflect the cost of your treatment if your hard times push you to get too involved with the word that appears on your upside-down screen."

Use the word list on this page to create problems of your own. When building a "calculator routine" for your training content, follow these guidelines for maximum impact:

1) Give each number in the computation a reason for existing (i.e. the number of days in a year, the number of letters in the company's name, the phone number of a financial expert, and so forth.).

2) Use a series of computations with different clever words (i.e. "giggle," "slob," "boss," etc.) to make the strongest impression. As each word changes into another word, the impact is heightened. Three changes seems to be the perfect series.

3) Although the word list doesn't contain any proper names, several common ones are possible. If you have a participant with the name of Bill or Lee or Bob, by all means use it to personalize the closing.

4) Don't be afraid to combine words. Add a decimal point to separate them.

The following words are some of those that can be made with the inverted numbers of a calculator. The required calculator number follows the word in parentheses.

| | | |
|---|---|---|
| BE (38) | BELL (7738) | BLISS (55178) |
| BEE (338) | BESIEGE (3931538) | BOGGLE |
| BEIGE (39138) | BIG (918) | (379908)(5507) |
| BELL (7738) | BILL (7718) | BOIL (7108) |

BOOZE (32008)
BOSS (5508)
EEL (733)
EGG (993)
ELIGIBLE
 (37819173)
GEESE (35339)
GLEE (3379)
GOOSE (35009)
GIGGLE (379919)
GLIB (8179)
GLOB (8079)
GOBBLE (378809)
GOGGLES
 (5379909)
HELLISH
 (4517734)
HIGH (4914)
HOBBIES
 (5318804)

HOE (304)
HOGGISH
 (4519904)
HOLE (3704)
ILL (771)
ILLEGIBLE
 (378193771)
IS (51)
ISLE (3751)
LEG (937)
LEGIBLE (3781937)
LESS (5537)
LIBEL (73817)
LIE (317)
LILIES (531717)
LOG (907)
LOOSE (35007)
LOSE (3507)
LOSS (5507)
OBESE (35380)

OBLIGE (391780)
OIL (710)
SEE (335)
SEIZE (32135)
SELL (7735)
SHE (345)
SHELL (77345)
SHOE (3045)
SIEGE (39315)
SIGH (4915)
SIZE (3215)
SIZZLE (372215)
SLEIGH BELLS
 (57738.491375)
SLOB (8075)
SOB (805)
SOIL (7105)

# 25

# An Odd Way to End the Day

Don't even breathe the words "In closing" during the final minutes of your session. Instead, try something like, "Before we're done here, I have something odd I want to show you." This statement piques participants' curiosity, instead of sending a verbal cue for subconscious shut-down.

Then go on to fulfill your participants' expectations. Select 11 participants (the number can be anywhere from eight to 15, depending upon your content emphases) to come to the front of the room. Line ten of them in a row across the front of the room and stand one off to the side next to you. As students come to the front, give each an 8½" × 11" sheet of paper (folded in thirds) to hold.

Address the person standing next to you with these words: "I told you that I wanted to show you something odd, and I'm going to. However, I'm going to ask you to do something odd, too. Imagine that the people lined up across the front of the room are numbered one, two, three, four, from left to right, up through ten. The odd thing I want you to do is to eliminate the odd-numbered people (1,3,5,7,9) and take their pieces of paper from them."

After the odd-numbered people have been eliminated (with a nice round of applause), take their pieces of paper and read each one (or have the group read them in unison out loud). Each piece of paper is actually a sign. On each sign is a negative behavior or action you, as trainer, specified must be halted or eliminated for effective workplace performance. (One suggestion is to take a behavior from each sub-topic.)

Ask the remaining volunteers to close ranks. Then address the person beside you again: "Once more, I want you to do something odd. Imagine that the people remaining in the front of the room are now numbered one through five (left to right). Now please repeat that odd thing, and eliminate the odd-numbered people."

Now the people numbered one, three, and five are eliminated. Only two people remain.

Take the papers from the eliminated participants and again read them to the others. Once again, the papers are signs showing other elements that need to be eliminated, based on your course content.

Have the two remaining people stand next to each other and again repeat the instructions to the volunteer. The two people left will be numbered one and two (from left to right). Again, you want the volunteer to do an odd thing by eliminating the odd-numbered person. The person on the left is asked to leave; his sign is taken and read to the group. Again, it is an element that needs to be eliminated for successful application of the content. Only one person remains.

The sign is taken from the remaining person. The volunteer and the remaining participant are both thanked for their help and sent back to their seats with a round of applause.

The remaining sign is unfolded and the entire group reads it aloud. It is your summarizing statement slogan for the session. It is that single most indispensable piece of advice that must be in place (not eliminated) if success is to occur. After everyone has read the statement, the trainer concludes the session by saying, "Now, isn't that odd?" Everyone laughs and the session is brought to a satisfying and fun conclusion.

The only requirements for this intriguing close is to have between eight and 15 printed signs. On all of the signs but one you should print in large type the elements that need to be ELIMINATED so that successful application of the content might occur. On one sign, print in large letters a concluding statement or slogan that captures the essence of what MUST BE IN PLACE for success to occur.

When you initially line up your participants across the front of the room, just make sure that this one special sign is given to the #8 participant. Then just follow the pattern above and that sign will always be the one remaining at the end. Now, isn't that odd?

# 26

# Three Points, One Page

When applying this closing exercise, try to take care of all housekeeping, evaluations, and announcements before moving into your closing. Then you won't be stepping on your own closing. When you are done, you merely need to say good-bye and send your participants on their way.

In preparing for this simple yet elegant closing, you will need to be able to summarize your content in three words. The first two words must start with the same letter; the third word can begin with any letter you desire. The time you spend selecting these words will reap rich dividends as you deliver your message, so choose well.

1.  To prepare, take a legal-size piece of paper and, holding the paper so that the long edges are horizontal, print a key content word on the front of the paper, large enough so that it crosses the entire page.

2.  Now fold the right edge of the paper across, so that all but the first letter of your first word is covered. Crease the page. Use the starting letter from the first word to start the second word, and write it on the surface you're now seeing.

3.  Finally, without unfolding the page, write your third key content word on the blank back of the sheet.

4.  In presentation, hold up the unfolded piece of paper showing your first word. Make appropriate comments and fold the sheet to display the second concept. After commenting on this aspect of your course, turn the entire packet over to reveal your final summarizing word.

If you're feeling particularly clever, you can make the exercise more complex. For this method, make sure that your first word STARTS with the same letter as one of the other two words, and ENDS with the same letter as the third word.

Prepare the first two words exactly as shown above. But instead of flipping the sheet to record the third word, unfold the page to its original position, and fold the left side of the sheet over until it covers all but the last letter of the first word you wrote. Then, when presenting, show and talk about the first word, and then fold the page to display the second word. Discuss this idea, then unfold the page and fold the right side over to show the third concept.

You will have closed with pizzazz, symbolically showing how ideas are linked together, and you will have visually held the attention of your participants, too—a powerful combination.

# 27

# Don't Let the Lights Go Out

I spoke with a trainer not too long ago who was listening at a remote site to an individual who presented himself as an expert in the field of distance learning.

The topic of this presentation was how to avoid participant passivity in distance-learning sessions. He was sharing ways to keep participants actively involved. However, from time to time the lights at the remote site would flicker, go out, and then come back on again.

The person telling me the story couldn't figure out what made the lights go out and then come back on. However, one time he did notice that when the lights went out, a person in the front row waved her hand in the air and the lights came back on.

Curiosity got the best of him and he asked the lady what was happening. The lady pointed to a box on the ceiling, indicating the presence of a motion detector so that lights in the room couldn't be left on accidentally at night. Whenever there wasn't any movement in the room, the lights would turn themselves off. She waved her hand to turn them back on.

Needless to say, with that lack of movement on the part of the participants, the presentation of the "expert" lost much of its credibility.

I couldn't help but wonder what would happen if motion detectors were mandatory equipment in every training room. Ever since that story, I haven't been able to conduct a training session without asking myself how many times the lights will go out. What do you think?

# Creative Thinking

# 28

# Making "Horse Sense" During a Major Change

If your participants are experiencing an organizational downsizing (or "rightsizing," as it is often euphemistically called), try this exercise to help them think more positively about what is usually a very traumatic experience in the life of any employee.

1. Give each team 13 wooden matches or toothpicks. Ask participants to build a model of six horse stables, as shown below. You can construct the pattern on your overhead platform to help the team get the idea.

2. Tell this story:

   *Once upon a time, there was a lady who owned six horses. She rented six stalls from a farmer, and housed her horses there for many years.*

   *The farmer, not a young man at the outset of our story, grew aged and eventually died. The farm was sold. The new owner had new ideas. He replaced the old per-stall rental arrangement with something more profitable—a per-board rental system. The new rates were incredibly steep—the woman could no longer afford to rent seven stalls. In fact, she would have to give up seven of the stall walls she had been using to house her horses. (At this point, remove sticks as shown, and invite participants to do the same.)*

71

*The lady's challenge was to move the remaining walls so that she could still house her six horses. She figured out a way to survive the radical reduction in resources. Can you?*

Give participants time to struggle for a solution. No doubt, someone will discover the successful answer. Creativity prevails!

*Solution:*

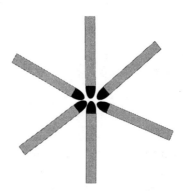

# 29

# Learning to Think

Trainers can now choose from a plethora of activities that help participants think more creatively in relation to problem solving. However, in many instances the left-brain processes need to be encouraged, as well. Many problem-solving situations require a high level of logical evaluation, blended with the creativity necessary for brainstorming.

I'd like to share two exercises you can try with participants in an effort to strengthen their ability to think logically.

1. Write the following on a flipchart:

   "There is at least one three to the right of a two. There is at least one three to the left of a three. There is at least one heart to the left of a club. There is at least one heart to the right of a heart. What are the three cards?"

2. Then set three cards (face-down) in the tray at the bottom of the flipchart in the following order, from left to right, as viewed by your participants:

   2 of Hearts 3 of Hearts 3 of Clubs

The challenge is for them to tell you the values of the cards in the tray simply by reading the statement you've written on the flipchart.
Have them work in teams for maximum interaction.

3. After the correct answer has been given, have participants try to define the process they went through in order to arrive at the correct answer. Explain that the logic they used to solve the problem proves they have the stuff to work through many complex work-place challenges they might be avoiding because they look too confusing.

Here's a second activity that strengthens the same faculties of logic.

1. Begin by telling participants the following story:

   *A boy and a girl are talking. "I'm a boy," says the one with black hair.*

   *"I'm a girl," says the one with red hair.*

   *If at least one of them is lying, who has which-colored hair?*

   *The answer is that they both lied. The boy has red hair and the girl has black hair.*

The way to help students think through this problem (and all problems they wish to solve logically) is by first asking, "What are all the possible combinations?" This is equivalent to the brainstorming phase in the problem-solving process. List all the possibilities; in this scenario, there are only four:

   1) The boy told the truth/the girl told the truth.

   2) The boy lied/the girl told the truth.

   3) The girl lied/the boy told the truth.

   4) They both lied.

2. The second step is to eliminate the possibilities that won't logically work. This corresponds to problem-solving stages, when the long list of possibilities is evaluated.

   The **first** possibility cannot be true, because we've been told that at least one of them lied. The **second** and **third** ones can't be true either, because if one lied about their gender in relation to the color of their hair, then the other one must have lied, as well. If just the redhead had lied, for example, this would mean both would have to be boys—unless the brunette lied, as well.

   Consequently, only the **fourth** possibility is logically acceptable: Both lied.

Exercises like these will help sharpen the "logic" skills of your participants. And they'll have fun, too.

# 30

# Mind Over Machine

Computers are beating champion chess players and even replacing human workers, so it's no surprise that the "human vs. machine challenge" is on the minds of your participants. This is particularly true if computer training is part of your training responsibility.

Students succeed in computer training when they meticulously follow the processes learned in the class. When the process and instructions are not followed precisely, disaster often results.

Dramatically demonstrate the power of a popular system and inspire participants to learn the system you'll be teaching by challenging two participants in your next training class to pull the calculator function of their computer up on their individual screens. You are going to ask both of them to do some computations using their computers; you will attempt to better their times using only your (unaided) mind!

1. Draw a two-column diagram on your screen, flipchart, or transparency. Label the columns A and B. These letters will represent the two participants you'll race against in this demonstration. One will be volunteer A, and one will be volunteer B. As you become familiar with this system, you could use participants' names in place of the letters.

2. Have participant A give you any three-digit number. The only stipulation is that the number must contain three different digits: i.e., 478; (the number 488 would not qualify since the digit 8 appears twice). Write the selected number under both letter A and the letter B. Assuming A's number was 478, your overhead screen will now look like this:

| A | B |
|---|---|
| 478 | 478 |

3.  Have spectator B volunteer a three-digit number again, with each digit different from the other (i.e., 743). Write that number on your overhead *below* the number already written under the letter A. Assuming the number given by participant B is 743, your diagram will now look like this:

| A | B |
|---|---|
| 478 | 478 |
| 743 | |

4.  It would only be fair that you, too, get to volunteer a number, so write a number of your own choosing underneath the number already in the B column.

    However, you get to use a secret process to select your number: Mentally subtract the number offered by B (743) from the number 999. In our example, you would write the number 256 in the B column because 999 – 743 = 256. (The numerically impaired may find subtracting from 1,000 and subtracting one from the result a bit easier to handle.)

    Your diagram now looks like this:

| A | B |
|---|---|
| 478 | 478 |
| 743 | 256 |

5.  Instruct your volunteers to multiply the numbers in their individual columns together and add these together for a grand total. Computer calculators may be used, but you will race them using only mental computation to get to that grand total before they do. Appoint a timekeeper to add to the dramatics, and start the race.

    Volunteer A will multiply 478 by 743 and get a total of 355,154.

    Meanwhile, volunteer B will be multiplying 478 by 256 and getting a total of 122,368.

    They will then need to check with each other and add together 355,154 and 122,368 to get a grand total of 477,522.

*Note:* You will always beat the machines, because you will be using the following secret two-step system:

1.  Subtract 1 from the first number offered by participant A. In this case, you would subtract 1 from 478, giving you 477. These are the first three digits of the grand total.

2. Subtract the first three digits of the grand total (477) from 999 (or again, from 1,000, then subtract one) and you will have the final three digits of the answer: 522.

The final answer is 477,522!

The easiest way I've found to present this is to work right on my overhead transparency (or computer screen in the front of the room), mentally arriving at the first three digits and writing these on the transparency. Then it's easy to mentally subtract those digits from 999 to get the final digits of the grand total.

As soon as you get the answer written on the overhead, shout "STOP!" and ask the timekeeper for the time. (To get a little extra mileage from this, act discouraged as if it took you longer than usual, and offer to try again right after the next break. You can bet that they'll all be back on time!)

No need to reveal your secret. Just tell the class you accurately applied a system, and that they, too, can accomplish even greater wonders if they learn to use the systems in front of them—their computers.

If you keep the process of this dramatic demonstration a secret, I guarantee that good things about your course will spread like wildfire, as students share their amazement with others not in attendance.

# 31

# "Twisted" Thinking Saves the Day

I call this one "Baffling Blocks." The trainer distributes a sheet of paper upon which a series of five boxes are drawn. Inside each box is a different capital letter. The letters are W, E, U, L, A.

*The challenge is this:* The participants must cut out the boxes from the handout and arrange the five letters in a single row so they spell a common English word. No proper names allowed.

The participants' mental processes become quite predictable. Although at first glance this looks like a simple assignment, the participants will soon find themselves struggling to find a common English word that can be spelled with those letters. Eventually, they will begin experimenting.

The first attempt will usually be to turn the W upside down and begin working with it as an M. However, that still yields no word. The next step is to turn the U on its side so that it becomes a C. Someone will usually shout out the word "CAMEL!" Others will wonder how in the world they arrived at the word "camel," and then everyone will follow suit.

The process parallels every group problem-solving exercise, and consequently is particularly appropriate in setting the stage for a group problem-solving or focus group session.

*The process begins with a definition of the problem, then comes brainstorming, and then experimentation with possibilities. Finally, the group agrees on the solution that best solves the problem.*

An additional lesson: We mustn't get stuck trying to find the one and only perfect solution. Many times there is more than one solution. I tell my students that this exercise taught me to remember this point: Looking for the perfect solution often prevents us from finding the best solutions. One participant creatively used the letters W, E, U, L, A just as they were, and spelled the word VALUE. I couldn't understand how he did this until I walked over to him and noticed that he had placed half of the W block underneath the A block, successfully transforming the W into a V by hiding half of it. Now, *that's* creativity!

# 32

# Possible Impossibilities

If students are intimidated or apprehensive about your subject matter, one good message to deliver at the outset is the following: nothing's impossible. And if things are not impossible, they may even be simpler than they sound. Many things SEEM impossible—the key word here is SEEM.

Here are some "impossible" brainteasers that nicely illustrate that point:

- "I turned off a light in my bedroom and managed to get to bed before the room was dark. The light switch is 10 feet from my bed."

   Someone in your class will think of the solution: It was the middle of the afternoon when he turned off the light. Of COURSE the speaker could get to bed before the room was dark! The assumptions we make trap us every time.

- "My friend's uncle was reading a book when his wife turned off the light. He went right on reading. How was that possible? In the light of the previous riddle (no pun intended), I know what you're thinking. But when the light was turned off, it was completely dark in the room and the uncle did not have a flashlight or match to provide any light, either!"

   Do you think anyone in your group will suggest that the uncle was reading braille?

Here's a final one that you could even give as a personal story.

- "This morning my wedding ring fell into my coffee. The cup was full, but my ring didn't get wet. Can you explain this? There was nothing wrapped around the ring to keep it dry."

   If this stumps participants, you can go on to explain that it was instant coffee and the water hadn't been added yet.

Transfer these and other brainteasers onto transparencies and keep them at hand for use throughout the session. They're handy when you transition into and out of breaks. And every time you use one, you will have made an important point about how the impossible oftentimes only looks (or sounds) impossible—an important motivational emphasis to keep in front of your students.

# Review

# 33

# Off to the Races

A review, by definition, is about old stuff. People have discussed the materials already and aren't always anxious to do so again. I add a jolt of excitement to reviews with "Off to the Races!," an exercise that brings all the excitement of the track into the classroom.

1. Prepare a deck of index cards with a review question on each card. Give each table a number. These will be teams for purposes of the game. Number each card to correspond with one of the teams' numbers. You'll want at least five question cards per team for maximum excitement.

2. Create a "race track." This can be done using a flipchart or a transparency. The track has a starting line and a finish line, and four squares between the two for each team. Whether the track is oval or straight is up to you.

   You'll also need some small markers to signify the position of each team's horse. Dimes work well on the overhead. Little horses cut out of the sticky part of Post-it notes work well on hanging charts.

   If you have the room, why not lay out the race track with masking tape right on the floor of your training room, and select participants from each team to be the "horses"?

3. You're ready to begin. Turn on some energizing music to set the mood, shuffle the deck of cards, and position the horses at the starting line.

4. Draw a card. Note the number on the card: This indicates which team will attempt to answer the question. A correct answer results in the team's horse moving forward one square. This continues until a team answers its fifth correct question and crosses the finish line. (A "champion's purse" can add some excitement and incentive to the race.)

That can be fun in itself, and can be used more than once (after each course segment, for example, as a periodic energizer). Students actually begin to look forward to a review.

But if you'd like to add a little extra flair to your session, demonstrate that you can magically predict the outcome of the race. You'll need a larger deck of review questions for this to work, but if you have about 60 question cards, it works perfectly.

Before the race begins, brag a little about your prowess at the track and how others often come to you for tips on the horses. Baiting your participants a little with this brag will help draw them into the event even more. Offer to demonstrate. Thoughtfully look over all the teams and then secretly write a prediction on a piece of paper. Fold it up and give it to a participant for safekeeping. Be sure to write the number of the only team that has five question cards in your secret top stack.

If your race track has four squares between the starting line and the finish line, stack the top of your face-down deck with a set of cards that has four question cards for each of the teams, with the exception of one team. That team has five question cards in that secret stack. So, if you have five teams, you will deliberately place 21 cards at the top of deck—four for each of the teams not slated to win, and five for the future winner.

When you get ready to have the deck shuffled, casually give this special stack to one person to shuffle and then casually divide the remainder of the question deck among three other participants. The apparent reason that you're dividing the deck before shuffling is the size of the deck and how unwieldy it would be for one person to shuffle that many cards. It also creates an illusion of fairness, since there's no way you as the trainer can manipulate the outcome, because you never shuffle the cards.

When reassembling the deck of question cards, just make sure that your special stack gets put back on top of the face-down deck. As you can now see, when they turn cards over from the top of the face-down deck, it will be impossible for the teams with only four cards in that top secret stack to win before the team with five cards in the stack rides their horse across the finish line to victory.

Regardless of how these cards are shuffled, the team you selected to win is guaranteed to get five questions, while any competitor can only hope to get four. After seeing your accuracy, your participants will soon beg you to accompany them to the track the next time they go.

*Note:* Your prediction will not hold true if the designated winner fails to answer each question correctly. Usually this is not a problem with team reviews, where cooperation almost always leads to a correct response.

Note also how this review game successfully combines the element of chance (the luck of the draw) with knowledge (the answering of the question). Seek to incorporate those two components in all of your review competitions and you will take the sting out of losing and the boast out of winning. It helps keep training competition fun!

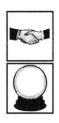

# 34

# The Flu Review

Sometimes you're lucky, and your trainees are *all* strangers to one another. That's not often the case. Most times, everyone in the group comes from a single department or work site except, perhaps, one or two participants, who don't know another soul in the room. And what about those situations where one person just doesn't seem to fit in? How do you help a participant who might be on the outside of the group feel more a part of what's going on?

One technique I've used is to involve the outside person in one of my review activities, serving as a "secret assistant." I call this "The Flu Review" for reasons that will soon be apparent.

After listing key content emphases on a flipchart, I tell the group that I will now do a little mind reading. I have their interest immediately.

I tell them I will turn my back while they silently decide as a group which content item on the flip chart to select as the "target item." After turning around, I will attempt to identify the item they select.

One of the participants volunteers to come to the front and serve as a silent facilitator during the selection process. I turn my back. The group silently selects one item. When I turn around, I ask participants to mentally think "stop" whenever my index finger touches the content item they selected.

As I move my index finger over the surface of the flipchart, I suddenly stop and confidently state that I'm now touching their selected content area. If they can't figure out how I do it, I might even do it several times during the day. I never miss, and it drives them crazy. And each time, we then review the item the group selects.

The secret takes us back to our initial question. During a break, I secretly ask the person who feels on the outside of the group to help me in a little demonstration. I explain the upcoming exercise, and ask this participant to simply sniff when my finger touches the item the group selects. This sniff doesn't need to be loud at all. When you're listening for it, you'll hear it every time.

The person who helps you feels like he's "in the know," and when you finally explain to your group how you did it, he becomes an instant star. And you reviewed content, too—not a bad combination!

# 35

# Charts of Wonder

A review, by nature, is one of the trainer's greatest and most frequent challenges. It covers topics that have already been discussed. It takes place at the end of the day or the session, when minds are wandering. And its frequent application makes it seem, at times, monotonous. It's not an exaggeration to say that you can't have *too many* review tricks in your training bag.

Put an illusionary sheen of mind-reading at the end of a training segment, and participants won't realize they're facing the ho-hum review monster. Here's one way:

1. Tell your students you're telepathic—that you know every thought they've entertained since they entered the room. Tell them you'll prove it.

2. Use any method you like to collect up to 100 course-related terms or ideas from students. You could make each student responsible for gleaning three words from a particular page of materials, for example.

3. Display these "content items" for the students. Consider letting participants tape the items onto a flipchart page while you provide a brief overview of the terms or ideas they post, or ask them to come forward and record their own contributions on a transparency. (This step and the one before are where much of the real review action takes place, but anticipation of the upcoming trick draws their attention from that fact.)

4. Number the items and ask a volunteer to come to the front of the room and concentrate on one of the numbered items. Provide the volunteer with a set of the seven labeled cards displayed here, with instructions to identify the cards containing the secret number and then return them to you.

5.  Identify the secret item, and provide an overview of the concept indicated. Repeat several times and then explain the trick, provide "magic cards" to participants, and let them review in pairs.

*Here's how to it works:* As the volunteer returns a card on which her selected number appears, observe the number that's in the upper left hand corner of each returned card. Adding those numbers together reveals the number of the secretly chosen item.

Let's say that the volunteer selects review item 37 from your flipchart listing. She would look over the six cards and hand you only the cards on which the number 37 appears—cards A, C, and F.

As the cards are returned, you add the numbers in the upper left-hand corner of those cards (1, 4, and 32). The total tells you that the person is thinking of content item 37. You then go on to describe that concept.

Here are some guidelines for making this most effective:

1.  Make sure that the person doing the mind-reading doesn't merely state the number of the thought-of item (there's no review in that approach). They need to describe the concept of the thought-of number.

2.  Make sure you emphasize that the volunteer must hand you back ALL of the cards bearing their selected number. Have them look a second time to be sure they've given you ALL of the cards with their number.

3.  If possible, have sets of cards for each of your participants. Even outside of class, they'll have fun showing the magic to others, and they'll be reminding themselves what a great time they have reviewing material in your class.

4.  Smaller numbers of items can be reviewed using only some of the cards:

    To review up to 15 content items use only cards A, B, C, D.
    To review up to 31 content items use only cards A, B, C, D, E.
    To review up to 63 content items use only cards A, B, C, D, E, F.

    When all the cards are used, you can review up to 100 different items!

| Card A | 1 | 11 | 21 | 31 | 41 | 51 | 61 | 71 | 81 | 91 |
| | 3 | 13 | 23 | 33 | 43 | 53 | 63 | 73 | 83 | 93 |
| | 5 | 15 | 25 | 35 | 45 | 55 | 65 | 75 | 85 | 95 |
| | 7 | 17 | 27 | 37 | 47 | 57 | 67 | 77 | 87 | 97 |
| | 9 | 19 | 29 | 39 | 49 | 59 | 69 | 79 | 89 | 99 |
| Card B | 2 | 11 | 22 | 31 | 42 | 51 | 62 | 71 | 82 | 91 |
| | 3 | 14 | 23 | 34 | 43 | 54 | 63 | 74 | 83 | 94 |
| | 6 | 15 | 26 | 35 | 46 | 55 | 66 | 75 | 86 | 95 |
| | 7 | 18 | 27 | 38 | 47 | 58 | 67 | 78 | 87 | 98 |
| | 10 | 19 | 30 | 39 | 50 | 59 | 70 | 79 | 90 | 99 |
| Card C | 4 | 13 | 22 | 31 | 44 | 53 | 62 | 71 | 84 | 93 |
| | 5 | 14 | 23 | 36 | 45 | 54 | 63 | 76 | 85 | 94 |
| | 6 | 15 | 28 | 37 | 46 | 55 | 68 | 77 | 86 | 95 |
| | 7 | 20 | 29 | 38 | 47 | 60 | 69 | 78 | 87 | 100 |
| | 12 | 21 | 30 | 39 | 52 | 61 | 70 | 79 | 92 | |
| Card D | 8 | 13 | 26 | 31 | 44 | 57 | 62 | 75 | 88 | 93 |
| | 9 | 14 | 27 | 40 | 45 | 58 | 63 | 76 | 89 | 94 |
| | 10 | 15 | 28 | 41 | 46 | 59 | 72 | 77 | 90 | 95 |
| | 11 | 24 | 29 | 42 | 47 | 60 | 73 | 78 | 91 | |
| | 12 | 25 | 30 | 43 | 56 | 61 | 74 | 79 | 92 | |
| Card E | 16 | 21 | 26 | 31 | 52 | 57 | 62 | 83 | 88 | 93 |
| | 17 | 22 | 27 | 48 | 53 | 58 | 63 | 84 | 89 | 94 |
| | 18 | 23 | 28 | 49 | 54 | 59 | 80 | 85 | 90 | 95 |
| | 19 | 24 | 29 | 50 | 55 | 60 | 81 | 86 | 91 | |
| | 20 | 25 | 30 | 51 | 56 | 61 | 82 | 87 | 92 | |
| Card F | 32 | 37 | 42 | 47 | 52 | 57 | 62 | 99 | | |
| | 33 | 38 | 43 | 48 | 53 | 58 | 63 | 100 | | |
| | 34 | 39 | 44 | 49 | 54 | 59 | 96 | | | |
| | 35 | 40 | 45 | 50 | 55 | 60 | 97 | | | |
| | 36 | 41 | 46 | 51 | 56 | 61 | 98 | | | |
| Card G | 64 | 69 | 74 | 79 | 84 | 89 | 94 | 99 | | |
| | 65 | 70 | 75 | 80 | 85 | 90 | 95 | 100 | | |
| | 66 | 71 | 76 | 81 | 86 | 91 | 96 | | | |
| | 67 | 72 | 77 | 82 | 87 | 92 | 97 | | | |
| | 68 | 73 | 78 | 83 | 88 | 93 | 98 | | | |

# 36

## Insuring Your Main Message

Psychologists tell us that the human mind finds it easiest to remember the first and last numbers in a series. The middle numbers tend to blur. The psychological principles are referred to as *primacy* and *recency*.

These principles can be applied to training: We believe our participants will remember the first activities of the class (openings) and the last activities of a class (closings). Therefore, it is a good idea to give these two components careful attention when you develop your plans for the training session.

Let's take a moment to define a "closing." When I use the word, I'm not talking about a review. That's still another component. I'm referring to the final "ta-dah" in which the trainer succinctly summarizes the main content emphasis.

By asking the question, "If your participants forget everything else about your content, what would you want them to remember?" you're well on your way to knowing the emphasis of your close. You'll want to be able to write that out.

Here's a closing technique that takes advantage of its fortunate place on the course agenda, by making your key message—the one idea you want EVERY student to take away—*the last words of the session.*

The trainer alludes to the fact that she or he has heard rumors about participants who have begun to file lawsuits against trainers for forgetting parts of their training that they later found out they needed back on their job. Sometimes it even affected their job performance so badly that they were fired. Consequently, the trainer explains, there are now insurance policies for trainers, to cover themselves in the event of forgetfulness.

As the trainer begins to close, she (or he) acts as if she can't remember what she wanted to emphasize. She scurries about looking for her "insurance policy." She finds it and displays its cover to the audience while reading the fine print to the class: "In the event that the trainer forgets the main emphases of his/her presentation, this policy agrees to pay each member of the class the sum of $1,000,000. This guarantee makes null and void all other guarantees either expressed verbally or in writing."

The instructor looks nervously around, then looks on the back of the policy. With a sigh of relief, she shows it to the class. Key points are shown in large, bold type.

Copy the next page or use your computer to create your own official looking document. Then fold it into fourths using the lines as your guides so that the official looking cover is on the outside of the folds. This should now look similar to an insurance binder. Open it up and print your text inside on the completely blank side of the paper. This document will now not only serve its acclaimed purpose—to ensure against trainer forgetfulness—but does so in a visual way to add extra emphasis to your key points.

# TRAINER'S INSURANCE POLICY

**In the event that the trainer forgets the main emphases of his/her presentation, this policy agrees to pay each member of the class the sum of $1,000,000.**

# 37

# Want High-Involvement Review? Bingo!

There are few review tools more flexible and entertaining than good old bingo. You can probably think of others, but this is one sure-fire way to put the game to work in the classroom as a combination review/evaluation technique. Here's how:

1. Design a five-square by five-square game card like the one pictured below. Participants will be writing in the squares, so make the grid as large as can be accommodated on a standard sheet of paper. Leave the square blank, with the exception of the center "free" space.

|  |  |  |  |  |
|--|--|--|--|--|
|  |  |  |  |  |
|  |  |  |  |  |
|  |  | **Free Space** |  |  |
|  |  |  |  |  |
|  |  |  |  |  |

2. Select 24 must-know facts or concepts from your session—the points you consider most important for students to retain. Before the class begins, formulate 24 questions that capture these points. Print the correct answers on slips of paper and place them into an envelope or other random-drawing vessel.

3. When you're ready to review, distribute the playing cards, one per participant. Read your questions out loud, one at a time, and ask participants to write appropriate answers in any space on their bingo cards, using each square only once.

4. Encourage participants to guess if they aren't sure of the answer. This helps you evaluate later, after your collect the cards. You'll be able to get a rough idea of where YOU may have erred—questions missed by numerous players—and you'll get an idea how well each student has understood the concepts you have presented. You'll also want every square filled in to prevent cheating by those who might write in answers during the post-game discussion.

After the cards have been filled, you can proceed one of two ways. Either go through the questions again and ask participants to correct their own answers, or take out your "answer envelope" and begin randomly drawing answers. In the latter case, ask participants to give you the corresponding question as you read correct answer—another round of review. Tell participants to cross out wrong answers and replace them as they are made aware of correct responses, and then make a mark through correct answers, as well. (Avoid punishing for failure, because *learning* is the goal.)

The first person to cross out five answers in a row, straight or diagonal, wins. For a more complete review of the 24 questions, change this so that the first person to get three or four complete rows crossed out wins. This increases flexibility in terms of time and content.

# 38

# Promise the World— Deliver a Great Review

Mystify your audience with this simple review. Since you'll be promising a lot, make sure participants understand it's all in fun, just in case you slip up somewhere and things get carried away!

*Advance Preparation:* Use your computer to print 25 labels. Beginning with 2, number the labels consecutively, from 2 through 26. Each label will also need to have a different prize listed on it. The prizes can be outlandishly lavish (a yacht, beachfront property, $5000 cash, and so forth), since you will only give away the prizes on card number 14 or 15. These two cards DO need to have prizes you can afford to give away, such as company mugs, keychains, or books that relate to the session's learning points.

Affix your labels to 25 different 3" × 5" index cards. Since you can use this set of review prize cards over and over again, you might consider laminating the cards to increase their durability.

Have a deck of playing cards nearby. You must secretly prepare this deck by removing the jokers, the instruction cards, and two of the aces. You will then need to arrange the remainder of the cards in the following order, without regard for the suits of the cards:

7-8-6-9-5-10-4-J-3-Q-2-K-A-K-2-Q-3-J-4-10-5-9-6-8-7-7-8-6-9-5-10-4-J-3-Q-2-K-A-K-2-Q-3-J-4-10-5-9-6-8-7.

For the trick that follows, count jacks as elevens, queens as twelves, kings as thirteens, and aces as ones. What you have done is stack the deck so that no matter where it is cut (the cut completed by putting the bottom stack atop the other), the sum of the top two cards will equal either 14 or 15.

1. Randomly distribute the prize index cards around the room to various participants. Each person who receives a card will get a chance to win the prize on his or her card. However, each must first stand and share an idea from the session that they actually plan to use back on the job.

2.  When that sharing is over (a rather painless way to review), it is time to award some prizes. Select a volunteer to come to the front of the room and cut the pre-arranged deck of cards, placing the bottom cut on top of the deck.

3.  Take the top two cards from the cut deck and hand them to your volunteer, who will add their values together.

4.  Thanks to your very ingenious stacking of the deck, you will find that the set of two cards will total either 14 or 15. Award the prize to the holder of the corresponding prize card.

You've reviewed your content (without ever once using the word "review") and generated excitement in the process! Your participants will surely appreciate that approach.

# 39

# Mystical Circles, Magical Learning

The lowly handout is often the trainer's last resort. My book RED HOT HANDOUTS presents 75 different tricks and optical illusions that can enliven even the most boring handout, making it more interactive and, consequently, more memorable. Here's a handout idea that isn't in that book. I call it "Flippit!"

Have your handout designed so that participants print the key emphases of your presentation inside a series of individual circles. Actually, there can be any number of circles. However, the size of the circles needs to be large enough so that once they are cut out, you can cover each one completely with the palm of the average adult's hand (approximately two inches in diameter seems about right).

After completing your presentation, have each participant cut out those content circles and get ready to learn a tricky game of mind-reading that makes a perfect closing.

Invite one person to the front and demonstrate the trick with him or her before explaining it to the whole group. Use the following script to guide you:

*"Place the circles down on the table. Place some with the writing facing up and some with the writing facing down. (Your volunteer arbitrarily decides the face-up or face-down position of each circle). I will then turn my back and you are to turn any two disks over at the same time. You can continue to turn any disks, as long as you always turn two at a time. When you are done, please cover one of them with your hand, and I will turn around and try to guess whether the one under your hand has the writing face-up or face-down."*

If another person tries it, she or he will only guess right 50% of the time, but you will win 100 percent of the time with the following strategy:

Before you turn your back on the circles, notice whether your volunteer has placed an even or an odd number of circles face-up, with the writing showing. If there is an odd number of circles with writing showing at the beginning, there will be an odd number of circles with writing showing at the conclusion of the turnings. If there is an even number of circles with

101

writing showing at the beginning of the trick before you turn your back, there will be an even number of circles with writing showing at the conclusion of the turnings. Using this information, you can deduce the position of the circle under your volunteer's hand by looking at the other circles that are showing on the table.

After successfully deducing the position of the circle under your volunteer's hand, explain the strategy to the entire group and have each participant try it with a partner at their table.

As you explain the strategy, you might even want to emphasize that winning always involves selecting the right components (your presentation's key emphases), and that you must use those components within the context of a properly designed strategy, if you want to win. Tell participants that you're about to teach them the strategy.

You'll be amazed at how those content circles suddenly take on new value to your participants, as they prepare to show this trick to others outside of the training room. This will reinforce your content each time. *That's* what I call training transfer!

# 40

# Even the Mistake is Predictable

Game shows are always a fun way to review content. Here's a way to use the tools of a game show to bring satisfying closure to your session.

You'll need a deck of numbered index cards, with each one containing a different review question from your session.

After having used them throughout the day in your reviews, secretly arrange the cards during a break so that all even-numbered questions are on the top of the deck, facing up. Add the number-seven question card to the top of the deck, as well. All odd-numbered cards except for number seven are placed at the bottom of the stack, face-down.

Now prepare three written predictions. Print them on 8½" × 11" sheets of paper, using large print so that most of the class will be able to read them when they are opened at the conclusion of the class. Seal them into envelopes.

The three predictions should read:

1. "There will be exactly _____ cards face-up." (The number in the blank should be the total number [amount] of even-numbered question cards in your index card deck, plus the one odd card you added to the top half of the deck.)

2. "There will only be even-numbered question cards face-up."

3. "I will make a mistake. The number 7 question card will also be face-up."

The outside of the envelopes should be numbered 1, 2, or 3, so that you will know the order in which to open the predictions.

In order to tap into the very powerful force of curiosity, you might want to hand out these predictions throughout the day, saying something like: "Here's a prediction about something that is going to happen later today. Would you please guard it for me?" That should pique some interest.

1. When you're ready to begin making your "predictions," invite two participants to come to the front of the room and, if possible, to sit down on either side of you at a table. You will remain standing between them throughout the presentation.

2. Place half of the deck face-down in front of one of the participants and the other half in front of the other. Unbeknownst to them, you will have placed the odd-numbered (minus number seven) question cards face-down in front of one player and the even-numbered question cards (plus number seven) face-down in front of the other player. Merely thumb through the cards face-up so that you can see the cards as you divide the cards into these two piles.

3. Invite either player to hand you a portion of his or her face-down cards from the top of one stack. The choice of who will be participating is up to the two players, as is the number of cards they hand you. This adds to the mystery of the magic.

4. Take the portion you are offered, turn it face-up, and then shuffle it face-up into the face-down pile in front of the other player. Again, invite either player to hand you a portion of their stack. Eventually, they will be handing you face-up *and* face-down cards. This doesn't matter. You will always turn the stack handed to you over and shuffle it into the other person's stack. You can repeat this process as often as you wish.

5. Finally, invite either player to hand you their entire stack of index cards. Turn it over and shuffle the entire stack into the stack of the other person. It will now appear to your participants that the entire stack of index cards is a randomly-shuffled mix of face-up and face-down cards.

6. Pick up the complete deck and look through it to make sure that the even-numbered cards (plus the seven that are face-up in the stack, which will either all be face-up or face-down). If you find that the even-numbered cards (plus the seven) are face-down, merely turn the entire stack over before replacing it on the table.

7. Push the cards over to one of the volunteers and ask them to separate the face-up from the face-down cards. When they have completed that task, push the face-down cards off to the side. You won't be needing them again in this presentation.

8. Now ask the other volunteer to count the number of face-up cards in the pile.

9. As unbelievable as it may seem, you are now ready to have your predictions opened and read, one at a time. They will all be correct!

10. Of course, after reading prediction number two, the group will be certain that you have failed, since the number-seven card will be among those found face-up. That will only heighten their excitement as they read your third and final prediction.

I never tell the participants how this small miracle is done, since I believe it would serve no purpose other than to satisfy their curiosity. This is the opposite of what I wish to do. Instead, I use this experience to conclude the session with words similar to this:

*"Interestingly enough, in this activity, I planned to fail. I would encourage you to do the same. As you take the information from this course and seek to apply it back on the job, you will not be 100-percent successful 100 percent of the time. No one in the human race ever is. By planning to fail from time to time, you will not be devastated by the experience, but rather will be better able to pick yourself up and keep on going. May that be your experience. Thank you for your participation in this course."*

Those final words will cue them that the class is over. Applause will usually ensue. Take your bow.

# 41

# Careful, or You'll Fool Yourself!

As you read through these instructions, try the activity yourself with playing cards in hand. You'll even fool yourself—imagine the impact on your participants!

At the conclusion of the class, the trainer asks each participant to take any nine playing cards from decks that have been placed on each table. They are told to shuffle their playing cards face-down and get ready to experience the most unusual card trick in the world!

After completing the shuffle, participants are told to look at the second card from the top of their face-down piles, and to remember that card. To help them remember, they can even place a mark on the face of the card, if they wish.

The trainer continues, giving the following instructions:

1.  Select a word that summarizes one of the emphases of the presentation—something you want to remember from the presentation. The word must have more than two letters, but not more than nine (the number of cards participants are holding). Share your words with others at your table, along with an explanation of why you selected that particular content emphasis.

2.  After you have shared the word, spell the word letter-by-letter. Count the cards one at a time from the top of their face-down, nine-card pile onto the table (one card for each letter in the chosen word). Drop the remainder of the cards still in your hand on top of the pile that is now on the table. (The trainer illustrates this process at the front of the room with his or her own nine-card pile.)

3.  Next, pick up the face-down pile of cards from the table and spell the word "MAGIC" (or any other five letter word), again putting one card from the pile face-down on the table for each letter. Drop the remainder of the cards on top.

4. Again, pick up the face-down pile and repeat step two by selecting one more idea from the presentation and condensing that idea into a single word. The summarizing word selected in this step must be at least three letters and not more than nine letters in length. Again, share your words with members of your table group. Spell the word, using cards from the top of their nine card pile, dropping the remainder of their cards on top.

5. Pick up your pile of cards and hold them face-down in your hand. You are now ready to find your first selected card. Spell only one more word. This time the word is "QUALITY" (any seven letter word will work).

Together, the entire room spells aloud in unison Q...U...A...L...I...T...Y.

Imagine students' surprise when every person in the room turns up the card that corresponds to the letter "Y!" They will be stunned to see their selected card!

To provide a little more flexibility in the selection of the final summarizing word, that word could also contain six letters. In that case, after spelling the word, you would have each participant turn *face-up* the top card on the pile still in their hand.

# Puzzlers for Presenters™

_____

# Introduction to
## *Puzzlers for Presenters*™

Within this final section, you'll find some of the very best overhead transparency masters from my Puzzlers for Presenters™ section on the Creative Training Techniques web site (www.cttbobpike.com).

Here are suggestions for maximizing the usefulness of these activities:

1.  Select a puzzle that you believe you can apply to your training content in some manner.

    By way of example, each puzzle will cause the group to move through a problem solving process involving some trial and error and some failure (many solutions will be tried before one is found that works). Mastering your content is not unlike that process. Success will not always come immediately. Let your participants know that and become comfortable with that fact. Any of the puzzles can be used to reinforce that point as the group reflects on the process it took to solve the puzzle. I've selected these puzzles with diversity in mind. I'm confident that other applications to your content will become apparent to you as you read through the descriptions.

2.  Make a transparency from the master and then use the transparency on your overhead to generate discussion at the beginning of a session or as participants are returning from break. For maximum energy, turn the puzzle solving into a contest. Offer a small prize to the first person (or table team) that solves the puzzle!

3.  Once a correct solution has been generated, apply the puzzle to your content and help your participants focus on the material you're about to present.

Everyone in your training group will now be on the same page. You will have refocused the group in a fun manner—replenishing that most essential commodity, group energy!

> **NOTE: For easy reference, the answer for each puzzler is hidden in the copyright notice at the bottom of the transparency.**

To celebrate her tenth birthday, Anne drove a nail into the trunk of an oak tree. Assuming that the tree grew 3 inches each year, how much higher would the nail be when Anne is 25 years old?

I have some pet fowl. They are all ducks but two, all geese but two, and all chickens but two. How many pet fowls do I have?

What are neither inside a house nor outside of a house, but still part of a house?

117

What is it that a rich man doesn't have, a poor man has plenty of, and when you die you take it with you?

What type of stone gets lighter the longer you carry it with you?

121

Can you name at least two
things that fall but never break?

Can you name at least one thing
that breaks but never falls?

What can you put inside a barrel
to make it lighter?
(Not helium!)

There are five words in the English language that end in "cion." Can you think of one of them?

When it's light, I'm dark; when it's dark, I'm gone; when I'm gone for good, so are you. What am I?

129

This morning my ring fell into my coffee. The cup was full but my ring didn't get wet. What happened?

When the day after tomorrow will be yesterday, today will be as far from Sunday as today was from Sunday when the day before yesterday is tomorrow. What day is it today, according to the above description?

Can you name three sports in which the winning players go backward?

What is it that you sit on, sleep in, and brush your teeth with?

What has eight wheels but is designed to carry only one passenger?

What is it that you throw out
when you need it and take in
when you don't?

141

Two bank robbers were captured, and one turned out to be the father of the other robber's son! How could it be?

Ten parts of the human body can be spelled with only three letters. Can you name them? (No slang needed.)

What is it that that was given to you, still belongs to you, that you've never lent to anyone, but that is used by everyone you know?

I purchase one for 30 cents; fourteen for 60 cents; and one hundred forty-four for 90 cents; each piece costs the same. What am I buying?

If it's not the day after after Monday or the day before Thursday, and it isn't Sunday tomorrow nor was it Sunday yesterday, and the day after tomorrow isn't isn't Saturday, and the day day before yesterday wasn't Wednesday, what day is it, according to this description?

151

# About the Author

Dave Arch, best-selling author and trainer of trainers, has written seven resource books for the training industry. His ideas can be found in Tricks For Trainers books and videos, as well as in his popular monthly column in the *Creative Training Techniques Newsletter*. Drawing upon twenty-five years of training experience, Dave travels for Creative Training Techniques, customizing and presenting four different participant-centered Train-the-Trainer seminars and keynotes (including the cutting-edge seminar entitled Creative Training Techniques for Distance Learning). Dave's clients include the Internal Revenue Service, Kimberly-Clark, the National Education Association, Canada Postal Service, and the Untied States Central Intelligence Agency.

# Other Training Resources
## by *Dave Arch*

---

Tricks For Trainers, Volumes 1 and 2
Tricks For Trainers Video Library (3 Volumes)
First Impressions/Lasting Impressions
Showmanship for Presenters
Red Hot Handouts
Dealing With Difficult Participants (with Bob Pike)
Trainer Bingo